BUG HUNTERS

by Jen Green

Series Editor Deborah Lock
US Senior Editor Shannon Beatty
Project Editor Caryn Jenner
Editor Pomona Zaheer
Designer Emma Hobson
Art Editor Yamini Panwar
Managing Editor Soma B. Chowdhury
Managing Art Editor Ahlawat Gunjan
Art Director Martin Wilson
Producer, Pre-production Francesca Wardell
DTP Designer Anita Yadav
Senior DTP Designer Jagtar Singh
Picture Researcher Sakshi Saluja

Reading Consultant Dr. Linda Gambrell, Ph.D.

First American edition 2015
Published in the United States by DK Publishing
345 Hudson Street, New York, New York 10014

Copyright © 2015 Dorling Kindersley Limited
A Penguin Random House Company
15 16 17 18 19 10 9 8 7 6 5 4 3 2 1
001—275327—August/2015

ISBN: 978-1-4654-3558-3 (paperback)
ISBN: 978-1-4654-3557-6 (hardback)

DK books are available at special discount when purchased in bulk for sales promotions,
premiums, fund-raising, or educational use. For details contact: DK Publishing Special Markets,
345 Hudson Street, New York, New York 10014 or SpecialSales@dk.com

Printed and bound in China.

The publisher would like to thank the following for their kind permission to reproduce their photographs:
(Key: a-above; b-below/bottom; c-centre; f-far; l-left; r-right; t-top)

1 **Corbis:** Piotr Naskrecki / Minden Pictures. **Dreamstime.com:** Antonioclemens (cla). **Getty Images:** Datacraft (t). 4 **Dreamstime.com:** Antonioclemens (cla). **Getty Images:** Datacraft (t). 5 **Alamy Images:** Robert Pickett / Papilio (br). **Dorling Kindersley:** Natural History Museum, London (br/Magnifying glass). 7 **Alamy Images:** James Caldwell. 9 **Corbis:** Piotr Naskrecki / Minden Pictures (b). **Dorling Kindersley:** Natural History Museum, London (tr). 11 **Corbis:** Michael & Patricia Fogden (t). 13 **Dorling Kindersley:** Peter Minister—modelmaker (tr). 14 **Dorling Kindersley:** Peter Minister—modelmaker (b). 15 **Dorling Kindersley:** Natural History Museum, London (cl, cr, crb). 16-17 **Dreamstime.com:** Luminis. 18-19 **Alamy Images:** Dynamic Graphics Group / IT Stock Free. 20 **Dreamstime.com:** Antonioclemens (ca). **Getty Images:** Datacraft (t). 21 **Dorling Kindersley:** Thomas Marent (b). 23 **Dorling Kindersley:** Thomas Marent (b). 24-25 **Alamy Images:** Odilon Dimier / PhotoAlto (Reproduced 12 times). 27 **Corbis:** Robert Pickett / Visuals Unlimited (t times). 28-29 **Corbis:** Ch'ien Lee / Minden Pictures. 29 **Corbis:** Norbert Wu / Science Faction (br). 34 **Dreamstime.com:** Pictac (c/Pencil). 36-37 **Corbis.** 38 **Dreamstime.com:** Antonioclemens (ca). **Getty Images:** Datacraft (t). 39 **Getty Images:** Konrad Wothe (t). 41 **Corbis:** Christian Ziegler / Minden Pictures (b). 42 **Dorling Kindersley:** Geoff Brightling / Peter Minister—modelmaker (br). 44-45 **Getty Images:** Glenn Oakley / Aurora (b). 46-47 **Corbis:** Hiroya Minakuchi / Minden Pictures. 47 **Dorling Kindersley:** Natural History Museum, London (bl). 48-49 **Alamy Images:** Premaphotos. 51 **Alamy Images:** Yvette Cardozo. 54 **Dreamstime.com:** Antonioclemens (ca). **Getty Images:** Datacraft (t). 55 **Corbis:** Ian Trower / Robert Harding World Imagery. 58-59 **Alamy Images:** Morley Read. 60 **Dorling Kindersley:** Natural History Museum, London (cl). **Dreamstime.com:** Antonioclemens (clb). 61 **Dorling Kindersley:** Natural History Museum, London (tr). 63 **Dorling Kindersley:** Kevin Schafer. 66 **Corbis:** Steven Vidler / Eurasia Press (cr). 67 **Corbis:** Murray Cooper / Minden Pictures (b); Galen Rowell (t). 68 **Dreamstime.com:** Antonioclemens (tr). **Getty Images:** Datacraft (t). 68-69 **Corbis:** Atlantide Phototravel (t). 74-75 **Alamy Images:** Roving Light Travel Photography. 75 **Dorling Kindersley:** Natural History Museum, London (clb). 77 **Alamy Images:** Magdalena Paluchowska (c). **Corbis:** Ian Trower / Robert Harding World Imagery (b). 78 **Dorling Kindersley:** Dave Rudkin / Peter Griffiths—modelmaker. 80-81 **Alamy Images:** Assorted Imagery By Phil (c). 80 **Dorling Kindersley:** Thomas Marent (br). 81 **Corbis:** Pete Oxford / Minden Pictures (br). 82-83 **Alamy Images:** Nicolas De Corte. 82 **Dreamstime.com:** Antonioclemens (tr). **Getty Images:** Datacraft (t). 84 **Alamy Images:** Will Steeley. 87 **Alamy Images:** Michael Doolittle (t). 89 **Dorling Kindersley:** Thomas Marent. 90 **Alamy Images:** Johner Images (l). 91 **Dorling Kindersley:** Natural History Museum, London (clb). 93 **Corbis:** Nigel Cattlin / Visuals Unlimited (b). 94 **Fotolia:** Vadim Yerofeyev (t). 96 **Getty Images:** Photodisc (crb). 96-97 **Dreamstime.com:** Luminis. 98-99 **Dreamstime.com:** Luminis. 100-101 **Corbis:** Rickey Rogers / Reuters (b). 100 **Dreamstime.com:** Antonioclemens (tr). **Getty Images:** Datacraft (t). 103 **Corbis:** Michael DeFreitas / Robert Harding World Imagery. 104 **Corbis:** 145 / Sylvain Cordier / Ocean (crb). **Dorling Kindersley:** Thomas Marent (bl). **Fotolia:** Ewan Chesser (br). 106 **Alamy Images:** Marc Tielemans (bl). **Corbis:** Christie's Images (bl/Butterfly). **Getty Images:** David Tipling / Lonely Planet Images (t). 109 **Getty Images:** Paul Zahl. 111 **Dorling Kindersley:** Natural History Museum, London (clb). 115 **Dorling Kindersley:** Natural History Museum, London (tr). 118 **Dorling Kindersley:** Barrie Watts (bc). 120 **Dorling Kindersley:** Natural History Museum, London (cb). **Dreamstime.com:** Eric Isselee (bc). **Fotolia:** Eric Isselee (bl). **Getty Images:** Morley Read. 121 **Dorling Kindersley:** Natural History Museum, London (bl). **Dreamstime.com:** Eric Isselee (c). **Fotolia:** Eric Isselee (cra). 122 **Alamy Images:** Brian Hagiwara / Brand X Pictures (cr). **Dreamstime.com:** Antonioclemens (tl). 123 **Dorling Kindersley:** Natural History Museum, London (tl). **Dreamstime.com:** Eric Isselee (bl) **Jacket images:** Front: **Corbis:** Darrell Gulin. **Dorling Kindersley:** Natural History Museum, London tc. Back: **Alamy Images:** William Gates / RGB Ventures / SuperStock tr; Brian Hagiwara / Brand X Pictures cla. **Corbis:** Pete Oxford / Minden Pictures tl, cl; Galen Rowell cra. Spine: **Corbis:** Michael & Patricia Fogden.

All other images © Dorling Kindersley
For further information see: www.dkimages.com

A WORLD OF IDEAS:
SEE ALL THERE IS TO KNOW

www.dk.com

CONTENTS

CHAPTER 1

WHAT ARE BUGS?

The Amazon Rain Forest teems with creepy-crawlies—small, scuttling creatures that some people call bugs. However, scientists use the word "bug" to refer to just one group of insects, which have piercing and sucking mouthparts. True bugs use their long, tubelike mouths like straws, to suck up liquid foods. The group includes shield bugs, cicadas, aphids, and bed bugs. Most bugs feed on plant sap. You will often see aphids clustering on garden plants such as roses. A few kinds of bugs are parasites, living on other creatures. For example, bed bugs live on animals or in their nests or bedding, and suck their blood.

Arthropods are a wider group of creepy-crawlies. This group includes not just insects but also spiders, scorpions, and centipedes. Arthropod means "jointed leg." All of these small creatures have legs with flexible joints and a body made up of several parts, or segments. Arthropods do not have a bony inner skeleton to support the body like we do. Instead, the soft body parts are protected by a hard outer case called an exoskeleton.

Scorpion under a magnifying glass

Spiders, scorpions, ticks, and mites belong to a group of arthropods called arachnids. All arachnids have eight jointed legs. The body has two main parts: a front section containing the head and thorax, and the abdomen or rear end.

Most arachnids are predators. They are armed with stings or poisons that they use to defend themselves and overcome their prey. Scorpions have a long, curling tail tipped with a poisonous stinger. Spiders bite their prey with poisoned fangs. The poison dissolves the prey's body to make a kind of soup, which the animal sucks up—it has no teeth to crunch up its prey.

Centipedes and millipedes belong to a different group of joint-legged creatures called myriapods. This word means "many legs." These minibeasts have long bodies that are divided into many sections, with legs attached to each. Centipedes can have as many as 360 legs. They are fierce predators. They hunt at night, racing after small prey that they kill with their poison fangs. Millipedes are plant eaters. Each section

Tarantula spider

of a millipede's body has two pairs of legs, not one pair like centipedes. The word millipede means "a thousand legs" but in fact, the highest number of legs on a millipede is 750.

Insects are by far the largest group of arthropods. They may be small, but scientists see them as the most successful group of animals on Earth—even more successful than the group of mammals, which includes humans. The variety of insects is quite breathtaking. Around a million different species have been identified so far. That means that three out of every four different animals on Earth are insects.

Insects are found almost everywhere on Earth—in deserts, woodlands, and grasslands as well as rain forests. They survive high on mountains, deep underground, in towns and cities, and in ponds and lakes. One reason for the insects' success is their small size. Being small means they can live in tiny spaces and don't need a lot of food. Some people see insects as pests because some kinds carry disease. Others eat crops or harm lumber. But insects are also very useful. They carry pollen between plants to fertilize crops and fruit trees.

They help make the soil fertile and above all, they provide food for many larger animals.

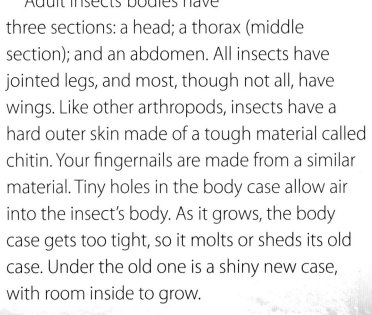

Adult insects' bodies have three sections: a head; a thorax (middle section); and an abdomen. All insects have jointed legs, and most, though not all, have wings. Like other arthropods, insects have a hard outer skin made of a tough material called chitin. Your fingernails are made from a similar material. Tiny holes in the body case allow air into the insect's body. As it grows, the body case gets too tight, so it molts or sheds its old case. Under the old one is a shiny new case, with room inside to grow.

Blue morpho butterflies

Scientists divide the huge supergroup of insects into smaller groups called orders. The insects in each order have a similar shape and feed and move in similar ways.

Beetles are the largest group of insects. There are over 350,000 different types of beetles! This group includes ladybugs, stag beetles, scarabs, and weevils. Like most insects, beetles have two pairs of wings, but the front wings are hard and rigid. They protect the delicate back wings, which are used for flying. Beetles come in every color of the rainbow—scarlet, blue, emerald green, or golden, like the rain forest beetle shown opposite. They also vary a lot in size. The very largest, the goliath beetle of Africa, measures a whopping 6 inches (15 cm) long, while the smallest would fit on a pinhead.

There are many other orders of insects. True bugs have about 80,000 species. The order of flies includes bluebottles and mosquitoes. Flies have only one pair of wings but are very skillful fliers. The order of grasshoppers and crickets

includes locusts, which gather in huge swarms and destroy farmers' crops. These insects have very powerful hind legs for leaping. The order of moths and butterflies contains many of the world's most beautiful insects. Another order contains wasps, bees, and ants, some of which live in large nest colonies. Dragonflies, earwigs, termites, fleas, and cockroaches are also insects. The variety is incredible.

Guide to Identifying Minibeasts

Most minibeasts, including insects, spiders, and centipedes, are arthropods, meaning "joint-legged," although others are mollusks or worms. The best way to identify them is to count the legs.

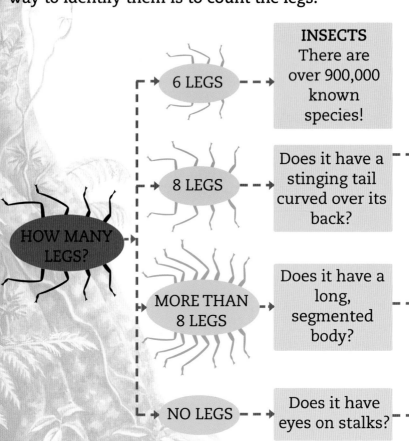

HOW MANY LEGS?

6 LEGS → **INSECTS** There are over 900,000 known species!

8 LEGS → Does it have a stinging tail curved over its back?

MORE THAN 8 LEGS → Does it have a long, segmented body?

NO LEGS → Does it have eyes on stalks?

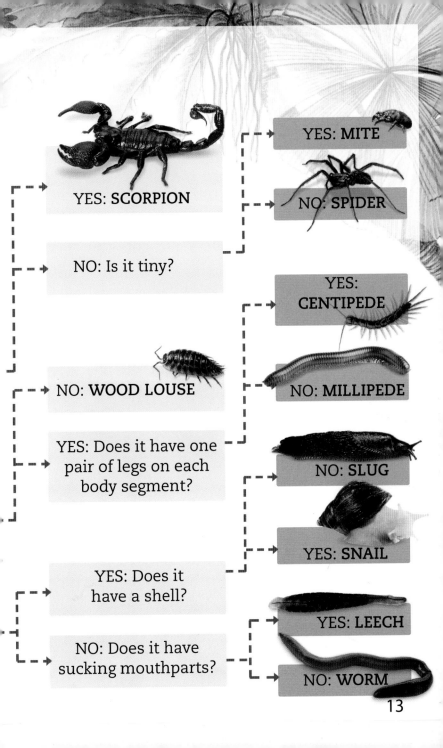

YES: **MITE**

NO: **SPIDER**

YES: **SCORPION**

NO: Is it tiny?

YES: **CENTIPEDE**

NO: **MILLIPEDE**

NO: **WOOD LOUSE**

YES: Does it have one pair of legs on each body segment?

NO: **SLUG**

YES: **SNAIL**

YES: Does it have a shell?

YES: **LEECH**

NO: Does it have sucking mouthparts?

NO: **WORM**

13

BUTTERFLIES AND MOTHS

Butterflies and moths form the insect group *Lepidoptera*, or "scale wings." The tiny scales on their wings overlap and reflect light, producing beautiful colors and patterns.

ANATOMY

Like all adult insects, butterflies and moths have three body sections: head, thorax (middle section), and abdomen (rear). The antennae are on the head. Butterflies and moths use their tube-shaped mouthparts, called a proboscis, to drink sugary liquids.

Antennae

Head

Proboscis

Thorax

Abdomen

BUTTERFLY OR MOTH?

Of roughly 140,000 species of moths and butterflies, only about 20,000 are butterflies. The rest are moths. How do you tell them apart?

BUTTERFLY
- Wings are often brightly colored
- Slim body with little hair
- Antennae have club tips (tiny knobs)
- Rests with wings upright
- Active by day

MOTH
- Wings are often dull colors
- Fat hairy body
- Antennae lack club tips
- Rests with wings flat
- Active at dusk / night

BLUE MORPHO BUTTERFLY

The wingspan of the blue morpho is 5–8 inches (12–20 cm) across. It comes in a variety of patterns and shades of blue. This butterfly is a prime target for collectors.

MOSQUITOES

The *Anopheles* mosquito is the world's deadliest animal, killing more than one million people annually. These insects can transmit malaria and other dangerous diseases as they drink blood.

MOST ACTIVE: evening, night, dawn

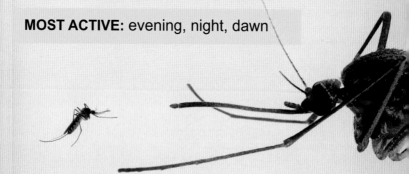

FEEDING

Female mosquitoes drink blood to obtain the protein they need to lay eggs. They pierce the victim's skin with their needlelike mouthparts, and suck up blood like a syringe. A special saliva is injected to prevent the victim's blood from clotting as they suck.

ACTION

- Take antimalarial pills.
- Use jungle-strength insect repellent and keep your body covered.
- Sleep under a mosquito net.
- Cover your face with mosquito netting attached to your sunhat.
- Don't camp near still water where mosquitoes breed.
- Never scratch insect bites— it will make them more itchy, and can lead to infection.
- If insect repellent runs out, cover exposed skin with mud. A smoky fire also deters mosquitoes.

PRAYING MANTIS

A praying mantis could easily be mistaken for a leaf. But this fearsome insect is skilled at stalking its prey or simply lying in wait for a meal. Its quick reflexes help the mantis trap its prey with strong front legs. The mantis then uses the spikes on its front legs to pin the prey in place in order to eat it.

CHAPTER 2

HOW INSECTS LIVE

Insects thrive in rain forests and many other places on Earth because of their varied feeding habits. The million or so species eat a huge range of different foods. About half of all insects eat plants. This could be leaves, stems, or roots, or it could be pollen or nectar from flowers.

Insects feed in two main ways, and their mouthparts are shaped to suit their way of feeding. Some have powerful jaws that they use to bite and crunch solid food. In other species, the mouthparts form a long, flexible tube that is used to suck up liquid foods such as plant sap—or even blood.

Butterflies such as these zebra swallowtails sip nectar—a sweet, sugary liquid found in flowers. The butterfly's mouthparts form a long, thin tube called a proboscis. Most of the time you can't see this because it is tightly coiled beneath the insect's head. But when it feeds, the butterfly uncoils and stretches out its little tube. Have a look next time you see a butterfly land on a flower.

Not all insects are plant eaters. Some feed on things that are dead or dying. This could be dead leaves, rotten wood, or the body of a dead animal, such as a rat. These insects are called scavengers, and they play a vital role in disposing of debris that would otherwise carpet the forest in a layer several feet deep!

Other insects, including fleas and mosquitoes, are parasites: they live on the bodies of larger animals and feed on their blood. Their victims are mainly warm-blooded animals—birds or mammals, including humans. As they fly or hop from one victim to another, insects such as mosquitoes can spread dangerous diseases.

Yet other insects are predators. They survive by killing and eating other animals. They mostly target other minibeasts, such as insects or millipedes, but a few go after larger prey, such as slugs and worms. Insect predators have senses finely tuned for hunting, and powerful jaws or legs for killing their prey.

Praying mantises like the one below use stealth to catch their prey. This large insect lies in wait for passing minibeasts. The colors and patterns on its legs, head, and body exactly match the flowers or leaves where it hides. It keeps completely still. Only the eyes move as they track the prey. When an unsuspecting insect comes into range, SNAP! The mantis pounces at lightning speed. It snatches up its prey in its spiny front legs, holds it firmly, and proceeds to eat it alive.

Most, but not all, insects can fly. They were the first animals to take to the air, an incredible 350 million years ago. The ability to fly allows insects to escape their enemies and reach food other animals cannot reach, such as pollen and nectar high in trees. Most insects have two pairs of wings. In butterflies, the front and hind wings overlap and flap together. Other insects, such as dragonflies, can move their front and back wings separately, which makes them fast and skillful fliers.

Some insects use the power of flight to make long, regular

journeys called migrations. They may travel to escape the cold of winter, reach new food sources, or find a good place to lay their eggs.

In the summer, monarch butterflies hatch in the United States and Canada. In the fall, they flutter south. Sometimes, the butterflies cover up to 80 miles (128 km) a day on their way to Mexico, where they spend the winter hibernating on trees. In the spring, they head north again.

Insects that cannot fly have other ways of getting around. They usually have strong legs and may be fast runners. Or they may live in water and be strong swimmers. If they live underground, their legs will be suited to tunneling through the soil. Fleas and crickets have strong back legs which they use to make giant leaps. A flea can leap eight inches (20 cm) in the air—130 times its own height. If you were that good at leaping, you could jump about 500 feet (152 m) in the air!

Insects are a very ancient group of animals. They have lived on Earth for over 400 million years. They appeared before the dinosaurs and survived long after dinosaurs died out. For an insect species to survive, the adults must breed successfully to reproduce their kind. Almost all insects breed by laying eggs, which they do after mating. They attract their mates with special colors, scents, or sounds.

A few types of insects can breed without mating or laying eggs. Female aphids can give birth to young that are exact copies of themselves without mating. This means they can breed very fast.

Many different kinds of animals feed on insects. Adult insects can fly, jump, or run fast to escape predators such as birds. However, young insects have no wings. They cannot fly or move fast, so how do they escape their enemies?

Many insects do so by hiding. The colors and patterns on their bodies exactly match the leaves, flowers, or bark on which they feed, so their enemies don't see them. This natural disguise is called camouflage.

Some young insects defend themselves with poison. They absorb poison by feeding on poisonous plants. They smell and taste so nasty that predators will not touch them. Others are camouflaged to look like unpleasant things, such as droppings. No bird will eat its own droppings, so this is a good disguise! Some caterpillars, like this morpho butterfly caterpillar, have spines or stinging hairs that make them a prickly or painful mouthful, so birds leave them alone.

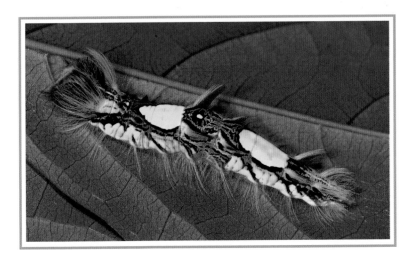

Insects are incredibly abundant—not just in rain forests but in many other places. In some parts of Earth's surface, over 1,000 insects live in just one square foot of ground. Part of the reason for this success is that insects are cold-blooded. This means that an insect's body temperature is about the same as its surroundings. It warms up by basking in the sunshine, and cools down by flying or crawling into the shade. Insects cannot keep their bodies at an even temperature like we can, so many die off in cold weather. But being cold-blooded means they need less energy than warm-blooded animals such as mammals, so they need a lot less food.

Insects such as bees and butterflies are active by day. Other species, such as moths and cicadas, are nocturnal—they move around at night. Their senses are tuned to finding food in darkness. They also need to track down others of their kind, so that they can mate.

Many insects that are active by day use bright colors to attract their mates, but colors don't show up in darkness. Night-active insects use sounds or smells instead. Cicadas and crickets make loud chirping sounds to attract their mates. Moths give off powerful scents.

Fireflies like the ones in this picture use lights to attract their partners. They mix two chemicals in their abdomen to give off little pulses of greenish light. Different species of fireflies use different patterns of flashes, like their own private Morse code.

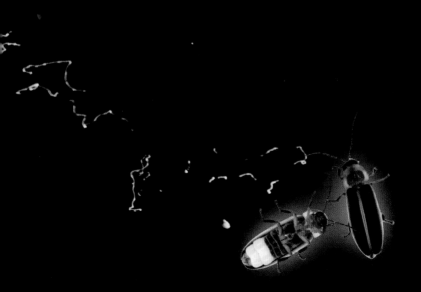

Insect Life Cycles

Almost all insects reproduce by laying eggs, but these eggs then develop into adults in two different ways: gradually (incomplete metamorphosis); or through complete transformation (metamorphosis). Most insects abandon their eggs after laying them.

INCOMPLETE METAMORPHOSIS

Grasshoppers, dragonflies, and termites hatch from eggs as nymphs, which resemble small, wingless adults. As they grow and cast off their outer layer, the wings sprout and grow, and eventually the insect becomes an adult.

Life cycle of the Southern Hawker dragonfly

METAMORPHOSIS

Bees, butterflies, and beetles hatch from eggs as young called larvae, which look nothing like the adults. Larvae may be legless grubs or caterpillars. When fully grown, the larva becomes a pupa. Inside the hard case, its body breaks down completely and is rebuilt as an adult insect. The winged adult breaks out of the case and flies away to mate.

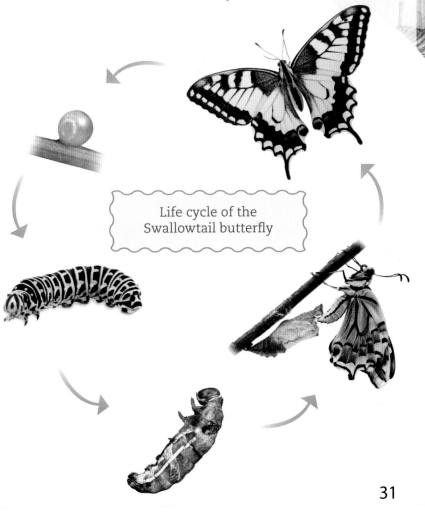

Life cycle of the Swallowtail butterfly

INSECT SENSES

Insects rely on their keen senses to find food, escape from predators, and survive long enough to breed. As well as sight, smell, hearing, taste, and touch, insects can also detect temperature, moisture, gravity, Earth's magnetic field, and ultraviolet light.

HEARING

Body hairs detect vibrations made by sounds. In various species, eardrums are located on the head, thorax, abdomen, legs, or wings.

TASTE

Taste organs are located on the feet of insects such as flies.

TOUCH

Hairs all over the body detect vibrations. Some insects have special touch-sensitive organs called cerci on their abdomens.

SIGHT

Large compound eyes give all-around vision. The many lenses are very good at detecting movement. Some insects also have small "simple" eyes on their heads that sense light and dark.

ANTENNAE

Main sense organs, used for smelling and feeling. Some insects also use their antennae to hear and taste.

SMELL

Vital for finding food and mates. Scents are detected by the antennae. Insects such as moths release special scents to attract mates.

Feed the Butterflies

Butterflies normally feed at flowers, sucking up sugary nectar with their long tongues, called a proboscis. By making a butterfly feeding station, you'll be able to observe them feeding up close. Instead of nectar, put out a sticky mixture of sugar and over-ripe fruit. Butterflies will love it! After dark, moths will come and eat too.

What you need

Over-ripe banana

Fork

Wooden spoon

Paper plate and string

1/2 cup (3½ oz) dark brown sugar

Mixing bowl

Saucepan

Pencil

2 cups water

1 Peel the banana, slice it, and put the slices in the bowl. Use the fork to mash the bananas into a paste.

 Ask an adult to help with cooking.

2 Mix the banana paste, sugar, and water in the saucepan. Heat until the mixture simmers. Let it cook so it becomes sticky and slightly runny. Turn off the heat and let it cool.

34

3 Make three holes in the plate with the pencil. Tie a piece of string around the plate through each hole.

4 Tie the plate to a low branch and smear on the paste. Now watch as the butterflies enjoy their meal!

Butterflies sense sweet food with their antennae and feet.

Butterflies will suck up the runny mixture.

MONARCH BUTTERFLY

Monarch butterflies can be found in many parts of the world. In North America, flocks of monarch butterflies migrate 2,500 miles (4,000 km) from Canada and the United States south to Mexico for the winter. Their wings measure 4 inches (10 cm) from end to end, and they flap at 300 to 720 times a minute, slower than most other butterflies.

CHAPTER 3

SOCIAL INSECTS

Most insects spend nearly their whole lives on their own. But some kinds live together in nests or colonies that contain many thousands of insects. For centuries, scientists have been fascinated by the cooperative lifestyle of these insects. Ants, termites, and some types of bees and wasps live together in this way. They are called "social insects."

Social insects are skillful architects. If the colony contains many insects, the nest will be large. It may be located high in a tree like the

Wasp nest

wasp nest shown here or it may lie underground. Some nests are round like basketballs. Others are long and thin, or shaped like a giant bell or a mushroom. Each species builds a different shape. Most nests are made of either mud or wood fibers. The wasps that made this nest scraped wood fibers from a tree or post, then chewed the fibers to make a pulp. Then they stuck bits of pulp together to shape the nest.

The nests of social insects are like miniature cities. Each insect has a particular job, which keeps the colony running smoothly. The different types of insects in a colony are known as castes. A large, fertile female called the queen lays the eggs. The job of male insects is to mate with her. Some colonies have soldiers, whose job is to defend the nest. If an intruder threatens a wasp or bee colony, the insects fly out in a swarm and sting the enemy. Soldier ants and termites have powerful jaws and can also squirt a jet of acid from their abdomen.

Most insects in the colony are workers. The workers have many jobs. They clean and repair the nest. They search for food, and look after the young insects. In bee and wasp colonies, the young hatch from eggs and grow up inside six-sided cells like the ones shown below. These little cells are made of wax, which comes from a gland in the worker's abdomen. The young wasps are legless grubs that cannot feed themselves, so the workers bring them food.

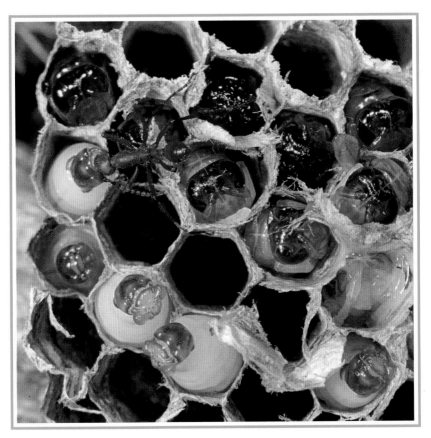

GUIDE TO SOCIAL INSECTS

The nests of social insects contain a maze of narrow passages. These lead to larger spaces that scientists call chambers. These mini-rooms have different uses. One contains the queen, while others may hold young insects, food, or even trash.

WASPS

- **Castes:** one queen; female workers
- **Nest:** often made of chewed wood fibers; may be large and intricate
- **Lifestyle:** adults feed on sweet foods such as rotting fruit; workers bring prey back to the nest to feed the young

TERMITES

- **Castes:** one queen and king; many thousands of male and female workers and soldiers
- **Nest:** some species build underground mud nests with tall ventilation chimneys; others build tree nests of wood fibers
- **Lifestyle:** feed on wood

ANTS

- **Castes:** one or more queens; many thousands of workers; soldiers who are sterile females
- **Nest:** usually underground; may contain millions of insects
- **Lifestyle:** different species of ants have different lifestyles—army ants are wanderers; leafcutter ants tend fungus gardens; slave-maker ants capture other ants as slaves

BEES

- **Castes:** one queen; males called drones; thousands of workers who are sterile females
- **Nest:** honeycombed with six-sided cells that contain food or young
- **Lifestyle:** workers collect pollen and nectar to feed themselves and the young—in so doing, they pollinate (fertilize) plants

If you look closely at a branch or vine in the rain forest, you may spot a long line of ants scurrying along it. Each ant carries a large piece of nibbled leaf, hoisted high above its head. These are leafcutter ants, and they are carrying leaves, which they have bitten off with their sharp jaws. The branch or vine forms a miniature highway, which the ants are using to carry the leaves back to their underground nest.

Back at the nest, the ants don't eat the leaves. Instead, they eat a special fungus, like a tiny mushroom. This fungus is found only inside leafcutter ants' nests, where it grows in a special chamber. The worker ants drop the nibbled leaves. They are picked up by another caste of ants called gardeners, who look after the

fungus. The gardener ants chew the leaves to make a compost, which they then feed to the fungus. The fungus thrives and grows on the compost, and all types of leafcutter ants then eat the fungus.

Leafcutter ants are also called parasol ants because the leaves they carry above their heads look like tiny parasols, or sunshades. If heavy rain falls, the worker ants drop the leaves and hurry back to the nest. Scientists believe that wet leaves could upset the conditions deep inside the nest that suit the fungus and make it grow.

Another type of ant lives in a society that is no less complicated than the leafcutter ants, but a lot more deadly.

If you take a walk in a tropical rain forest, you may come across an amazing sight: a small, dark stream flowing among the dry leaves on the ground. Look closer and you will see that the "stream" is really thousands of insects scurrying to and fro. A column of army ants is on the move!

The ants may be tiny, but in a group they are terrifying. Some scientists call them the ultimate predator of the Amazon—every bit as deadly as a jaguar, or even a poisonous snake. The marching ants are combing the forest floor for prey. Any minibeast that crosses their path is

unlikely to get away. The ants seize their victim, cut it up with their sharp jaws, and carry the pieces back to the nest. But army ants don't just target small creatures. They also kill birds, lizards, and any other animal that stays still for long enough. They have been known to kill dogs and even mules that were tied up and couldn't get away.

How do army ants work together to kill their prey?

Most types of social insects nest in one place, but army ants have no fixed home. Instead they spend their lives on the move, marching through the forest. On the way they set up temporary camps called bivouacs. Unlike most ants, these nests are above ground.

The worker ants cluster together and lock jaws to form a ball. In the center of the ball of living insects are the larvae and the queen—safe, warm, and protected from the weather. In the morning, the workers untangle themselves

and set off again in search of food.

Army ants spend about three weeks camped in one part of the forest. They return to the bivouac each night. Every day, they set out in a new direction to find food. After three weeks, many of the minibeasts in that part of the forest have been captured and killed. Food is now scarce. The ants march on and set up camp in a new part of the forest. Every minibeast in range of the new bivouac is in danger of being eaten by these terrifying ants.

The nest shown opposite was made by termites. These insects thrive in warm regions, especially in the tropics. They make their homes in grasslands and rain forests. There are about 2,000 species of termites. All are social insects, living together in large colonies. A big termite nest can hold up to three million insects!

Deep inside the nest is a large queen that lays eggs. She looks like a fat sausage because her body contains so many eggs. There are also soldiers with large heads, who defend the nest with their powerful jaws. All the other insects are workers. In bee, wasp, and ant nests, the workers are all undeveloped females, but termite colonies contain roughly equal numbers of males and females.

Termites feed on wood. In the tropics they do a lot of damage to wooden buildings and furniture. They can even eat right through the beams that support a house, causing the whole building to collapse!

Termite nest in a tree

Some types of termites nest high in trees. Others live in large nests underground with tall, slender "chimneys" rising above ground. Some termite chimneys are over 25 feet tall (7.6 m)!

These hollow chimneys create a flow of air, which cools the nest. The insects open or close passages leading to the chimneys to fine-tune the nest temperature.

Termites are blind. Nestmates mainly communicate using special scents called pheromones. Different scents tell the insects to clean or repair the nest, find food, or swarm out to defend the colony from danger.

Ladybug Home

Everybody loves ladybugs, with their bright spotted wings. Ladybugs are known as the gardener's best friend because they eat aphids and other tiny pests that cause damage to plants. Welcome ladybugs into your garden by making them a shelter.

What you need

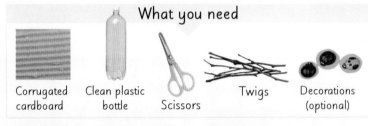

Corrugated cardboard | Clean plastic bottle | Scissors | Twigs | Decorations (optional)

1 Ask an adult to cut the top off a plastic bottle. Cut across the tubes of the corrugated cardboard to make a piece about the length of the bottle.

2 Roll up the corrugated cardboard as tightly as possible without crushing the tubes too much. Place the rolled-up cardboard inside the bottle.

3 Fill the hole in the middle with twigs that stick out a little from the end of the bottle. These are for the ladybugs to land on. Place the bottle in a dry, sheltered spot, such as in some shrubbery.

4 Ladybugs need to hibernate during the winter. Sometimes they hibernate in large colonies. This shelter will keep them snug, warm, and dry until they are ready to emerge in the spring.

Did You Know?
If frightened, ladybugs release a strong-smelling yellow goo to warn off predators.

CHAPTER 4

AMAZON RAIN FOREST

Imagine you are in an airplane, flying over a vast green forest. Tall, fluffy trees stretch out on all sides like a thick, woolly blanket. Far below, a broad, silver river winds through the forest. You are looking down on one of the world's most amazing places on Earth, the Amazon Rain Forest. This vast forest fills the basin of the Amazon River in South America.

Lush tropical rain forests grow close to the Equator. The sun beats down fiercely here, so it is always hot, and the air is sticky. Rain forests are so called because they get a lot of rain. Although many days dawn clear and sunny, clouds gather by midday, and rain falls on most afternoons, often to the rumble of thunder. Rain drips through the trees, splashes on the ground, and runs off into thousands of streams. These flow into rivers which eventually join the mighty Amazon.

The Amazon Rain Forest is massive, covering about half of South America. Rain falls here all year round, but the months from October to May are extra wet. Swollen by heavy rain, water levels rise. Streams and rivers burst their banks and spread out over the surrounding land. River dolphins, fish, and turtles swim among the trees where monkeys scramble when the forest is drier.

The Amazon Rain Forest is one of the last truly wild places on Earth. Whatever the weather, it's almost impossible to make your way on foot through this vast, tangled forest. The only way to get around is by boat.

For thousands of years, small groups of people have lived in the forest. Villages grew along streams and rivers that provide food, water—and a means of transportation. These people traditionally travel the river in dugout canoes, which they often hollow out by hand.

In the 16th century, the first Europeans arrived in the Amazon. Wishing to explore this enormous region, they too found that the only way to travel was by boat.

In the early 20th century, the first airplanes flew over the Amazon. Now many previously unreachable parts of the forest have a tiny airstrip where planes can land. Even when planes can land, however, much travel is still by boat because there are so few roads winding through the deep forest.

At ground level, the rain forest is a tangled mass of leafy growth. Trees thrive in the warm, wet conditions. Their huge trunks soar upward. High above the ground, each tree spreads its branches, twigs, and leaves to capture as much sunlight as possible. This forms a leafy layer that shades the ground below and makes some parts of the forest too dark for young plants to grow.

Mighty rain forest trees live for centuries, but even they do not last forever. In the end, these ancient trees grow old and die. Where a forest giant crashes to the ground, it creates a pool of light. Seeds hidden among the dead leaves sprout and grow. This is called germination. The slender young trees quickly grow upward. Each tries to spread its leaves in the sunshine, in a bid to become the next forest giant!

Tropical rain forests are among the most fertile places on Earth. Scientists believe that one-third of all the different plants and animals that live on land are found in the Amazon Rain Forest. This incredible variety of plant and animal life is called biodiversity.

For example, there is such a wide variety of trees that experts say you can walk through this ancient rain forest for an hour, and not see the same type of tree twice. What's more, each tree may have up to 50 other species of plants growing on it. Vines and creepers curl around tree trunks, while large, leafy ferns and bright flowers called orchids root on the mossy branches.

Animal life of the rain forest is just as varied as the plants.

Experts have counted 400 types of birds and 150 different butterflies in a tiny patch of forest just 2 miles (3.2 km) square. The waters  and forests of the Amazon hold around a tenth of the world's known mammals, fish, and frogs, along with hundreds of birds and reptiles.

The greatest variety of all is among the minibeasts—small creatures such as insects, centipedes, and spiders. Thousands of species have been identified and new ones are still being discovered every week. But experts say that they are just scratching the surface. They believe that only about a tenth of all the bugs in the rain forest have been identified so far. That leaves thousands and thousands more insects to be discovered, hiding on mossy tree trunks, high in the treetops, or among the leaves on the ground.

The plants and animals of the rain forest are all connected in a web of life. Every living thing depends on many others for survival. Animals rely on plants for food, but they also help plants spread their seeds far and wide, so that new plants can grow.

Plants provide the basic food of the rain forest. The green leaves and stems of plants work like miniature solar panels, capturing sunlight energy. The plant uses this energy to convert water and minerals from the soil and carbon dioxide gas from the air into leafy growth. This amazing process is called photosynthesis.

Plant foods include fruit, sap, leaves, and roots, as well as nectar and pollen from flowers. These are eaten by herbivores—plant-eating animals—from tiny bugs to sloths and monkeys. These plant eaters provide food for meat-eating predators. At the top of the rain forest food chain are the most powerful hunters of the forest, jaguars and eagles.

Howler monkey

LOCATION

Amazon Rain Forest, Brazil, South America

The Amazon Rain Forest is the largest remaining
tropical rain forest anywhere on Earth. It is located
in the river basin formed by the mighty Amazon River
and its many tributaries. This lush, green rain forest
contains more species of plants and animals than
any other habitat on land.

**Locations of remaining
tropical rain forests**

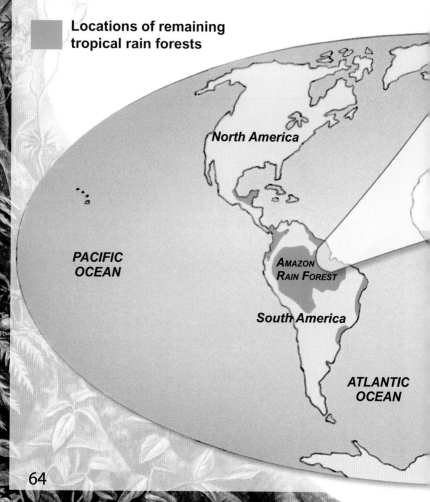

North America

PACIFIC
OCEAN

AMAZON
RAIN FOREST

South America

ATLANTIC
OCEAN

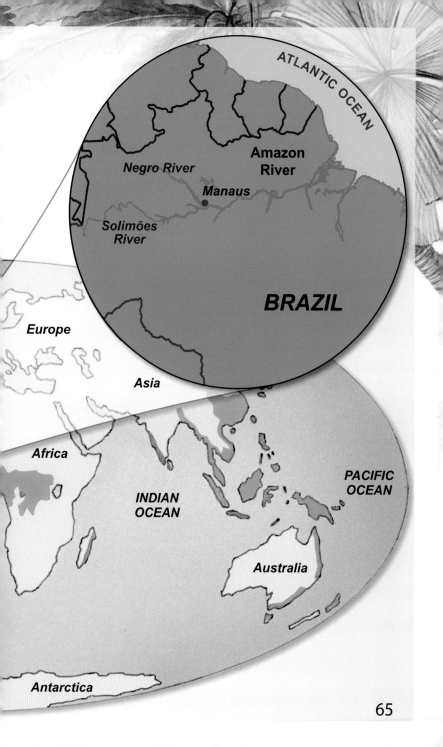

ATLANTIC OCEAN

Negro River

Amazon River

Manaus

Solimões River

BRAZIL

Europe

Asia

Africa

INDIAN OCEAN

PACIFIC OCEAN

Australia

Antarctica

Amazon Rain Forest and River

The **Amazon Rain Forest** is the largest on Earth, covering more than 2 million square miles (5.5 million square km), an area the size of the United States of America. About 60 percent of the rain forest is in **Brazil**, with the rest spread over seven other countries in South America.

AMAZON RIVER

A record one-fifth of Earth's total river water is carried by the Amazon River. It is the world's second-longest river at 4,000 miles (6,440 km) long. Over 1,100 smaller rivers join the Amazon as it flows east from the Andes Mountains to the Atlantic Ocean.

Amazon River

CLIMATE

- Temperatures stay at around 80°F (27°C) throughout the year—hot and sticky.
- The annual rainfall is a little over 80 inches (200 cm)—twice that of Washington, D.C.
- The rainy season is from October to May, with a drier season from June to September.
- During the rainy season, the river rises to flood vast areas of forest.

HABITATS

The Amazon region has many different habitats, including tropical rain forest, flooded forest, upland cloud forest, and tropical grasslands.

Amazon tropical rain forest treetops

Amazon flooded forest

RAIN FOREST HABITATS

Do you live in an apartment building? In cities, many people live in high-rise buildings. People live at every level, from the basement to the roof. Rain forest trees are like apartment buildings, with insects, spiders, and other creatures at every level from the ground to the treetops. Scientists who study life in the rain forest divide it into vertical layers called stories.

Most living things in the forest live high in the air, in the layer of dense foliage formed by the interlocking leaves of trees. This leafy layer,

called the canopy, grows about 100 feet (30 m) off the ground. Because of the warm, frost-free conditions in the Amazon, trees don't shed their leaves in the fall, so the canopy stays green all year round. Different types of trees bear fruit and flowers at different times of year, so there's always something to eat!

Leaves, stems, blossoms, fruits, and nuts provide food for clouds of flying and crawling insects. There are countless bees, wasps, ants, and butterflies. Larger animals live here too: flying creatures such as bats and birds, and skillful climbers such as squirrels, snakes, and monkeys. All of these animals feed on plants or prey on each other.

The canopy is not the topmost layer in the forest. Very tall trees called emergents grow even taller, spreading their crowns above the dense, leafy layer. The very tallest trees may be 200 feet high (61 m)—as tall as a 17-story building. Conditions are extreme here. The tall trees are rocked by strong winds, drenched by heavy rain, and baked by fierce sunshine. Even so, they are still home to hordes of crawling, flying, hopping, and buzzing insects.

The layer below the canopy is called the understory. The dense blanket of leaves above blocks almost all of the sunlight, so the understory is always dim and dark.

Trailing vines and creepers loop between the trunks of trees. Ferns, moss, and lichen sprout from lower branches. Plants called bromeliads also root on trunks and branches. Their waxy leaves form little cups that collect water. Tadpoles and insects such as mosquitoes grow up in these tiny pools.

The understory contains less life than the canopy above, but it is still home to hundreds of different creatures. Ants and termites use the vines as rope ladders as they climb up to gather food in the canopy. Some animals spend their whole lives in this shady layer and never drop down to the ground.

The ground level in a rain forest is called the forest floor. Conditions here are even more sheltered than in the understory. The mesh of leaves above allows only glimmers of light to reach the ground. The canopy also acts like a leaky umbrella, shielding the lower layers from moisture. After a heavy shower, it can take up to ten minutes for rain to dribble through the leaves and splash to the ground.

Very little grass grows in a rain forest. Thick vegetation grows in sunny clearings and along the banks of rivers, but elsewhere, few plants grow. A thick carpet of dead leaves covers the soil. Now you might think the soil in a rain forest would be rich and fertile, but in fact it is thin and poor, because plants take all the nutrients. The thin soil makes it hard for trees to root securely. Many trees grow sturdy roots shaped like rocket fins that branch sideways to support their enormous weight.

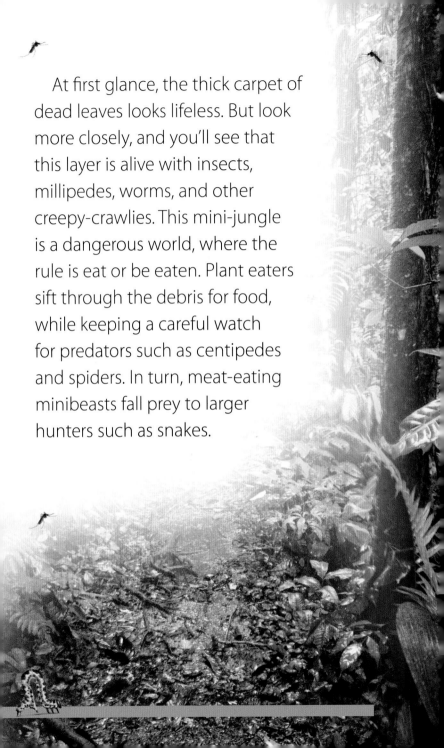

At first glance, the thick carpet of dead leaves looks lifeless. But look more closely, and you'll see that this layer is alive with insects, millipedes, worms, and other creepy-crawlies. This mini-jungle is a dangerous world, where the rule is eat or be eaten. Plant eaters sift through the debris for food, while keeping a careful watch for predators such as centipedes and spiders. In turn, meat-eating minibeasts fall prey to larger hunters such as snakes.

Here and there, the way is barred by a huge fallen tree trunk. Hollow trunks and mossy stumps provide homes for minibeasts such as centipedes, spiders, and insects. Some of these creatures spend their whole lives in dark places and never see the light of day. Their senses are suited to finding their food and escaping enemies in the dark. For example, some crickets that live in rotten trees have very long antennae. They use these long, sensitive feelers for tasting, smelling, and groping their way through the darkness.

Some wasps and beetles tunnel into fallen trees and lay their eggs there. When the grubs hatch out, they feast on wood. Other beetles and their young feed on the bodies of dead animals, large and small. Beetles, bugs, and also worms and fungi help break down the remains of living things. This helps return nutrients to the soil, where trees and plants use these nutrients to grow. In this way, insects and other minibeasts play a vital role in the life cycle of the forest. They help nourish plants, which in turn provide food for animals to grow.

How do insects and other minibeasts play a role in the life cycle of the forest?

Villages and towns in the Amazon provide a home for minibeasts. Before Europeans arrived, small groups of forest people lived in villages of thatched houses. They cleared patches of land to grow crops. They also hunted animals and gathered wild foods such as fruits, nuts, and honey. Insects and other minibeasts made their homes in these villages, which provided them with plenty of food.

In the 16th century, Europeans reached South America and began to explore the Amazon Rain Forest. They soon claimed large areas of land. They began to cut down trees for lumber and to clear the land to grow crops such as rubber. Some small villages on the Amazon grew into busy towns and cities. During the 19th century, the city of Manaus in Brazil grew wealthy from the export of rubber.

Whether large or small, all settlements in the Amazon are home to insects as well as people. Minibeasts move into our homes to feed on foods such as grain. Some hunt other minibeasts that live in houses, while others feed on things we don't think of as edible, such as wood, paper, and glue!

Layers of a Rain Forest

EMERGENT LAYER

CANOPY

UNDERSTORY

FOREST FLOOR

Scientists divide the rain forest into vertical layers called stories. Each layer has different conditions and its own set of plants and animals. Life is most plentiful in the canopy because food such as leaves, fruit, and flowers are abundant here.

EMERGENT LAYER—made up of the tallest trees.

Conditions: bright sunlight, wet and windy
Plant life: crowns of tall trees rising to 230 ft (70 m) or more
Animal life: monkeys; birds, including birds of prey such as the harpy eagle

CANOPY—made up of interlocking leaves and branches

Conditions: sunny, wet, more sheltered than emergent layer. The mesh of twigs and leaves prevents sunlight and moisture from reaching the layers below.
Plant life: crowns of rain forest trees, with ferns and orchids growing on branches
Animal life: monkeys, squirrels, and bats; birds; snakes and lizards; frogs; abundant insects

UNDERSTORY—the shady layer below the canopy

Conditions: shady, dry, and sheltered
Plant life: crowns of shorter trees such as palms; vines and creepers festoon tree trunks; shrubs and tall saplings
Animal life: sloths, jaguars; snakes; frogs; ants, termites, and other insects

FOREST FLOOR—ground level

Conditions: shady, dry, sheltered
Plant life: shrubs and saplings sprout in patches of sunlight; finlike buttress roots of trees; many types of fungi; dead leaves carpet ground
Animal life: ants, termites, beetles, and other insects; centipedes, millipedes, woodlice, spiders, and other arthropods; snakes; rodents, tapir, and armadillo

BLOG: INSECT CAMOUFLAGE

Here in the Amazon, insects are food for hundreds of different animals, from mammals such as bats and monkeys to birds, lizards, frogs—and also other insects. For many insects, the best defense is to blend in with the background, so predators don't see them. This natural disguise is called camouflage. Other insects stand out!

LIFESAVING DISGUISES

Leaf insects, mantises, and thorn bugs disguise themselves as parts of plants, such as leaves, twigs, flowers, bark, or thorns. They are incredibly hard to see, especially high up in the canopy. Predatory insects such as praying mantises use camouflage in a different way—they disguise themselves so they can surprise their prey.

Leaf bush cricket

Insects in other parts of the world use disguises too. Alder moths live in Europe and parts of Asia. Their larvae are disguised as bird droppings!

80

WHAT BIG EYES YOU HAVE!

Owl, peacock, and morpho butterflies, as well as some caterpillars, have spots on their wings or body that look like large eyes. These eyespots fool predators into thinking they are a large, dangerous animal such as an owl or snake, so the predators keep away!

Morpho butterfly

WARNING COLORS

Insects armed with stings, poisons, or foul-tasting fluids don't need to hide—it's better to be noticed. Insects such as wasps and poisonous caterpillars have bold yellow-and-black or red-and-black markings. Predators know to avoid these bright colors. However, some harmless insects have the same colors. They fool predators into leaving them alone so they aren't eaten.

Fungus beetle

81

CHAPTER 6

STUDYING RAIN FOREST BUGS

Scientists from all over the world come to the Amazon to study plants and animals, including minibeasts. There is every chance of finding creatures here that are new to science.

Many scientists would grab the chance to go on a jungle expedition. However, camp life is uncomfortable. The weather is always hot and sticky. The daily rain makes it hard to keep your clothing and equipment dry. There are also biting insects, such as midges and mosquitoes, so it's important to wear insect repellent, long-sleeved shirts, and trousers.

Rain forest camps have no comfy beds or air-conditioning. Most don't even have tents. Scientists sleep in hammocks slung between trees. A tarpaulin keeps the rain off and a mosquito net keeps out insects. Getting in and out of a hammock is tricky, but it's best to sleep off the ground, out of reach of creepy-crawlies.

It can take days to reach parts of the forest. Expedition members travel by plane to the nearest airstrip, then a boat to the camp. Often they spend weeks or even months deep in the forest. There may be a doctor at camp, but no hospital. A good first aid kit is essential.

The laboratory is the center of the expedition. This is normally a sturdy hut made of wood, with a thatched or tin roof. The space inside is lined with workbenches. Every scientist has a place for his or her research. Each is an expert in a particular type of wildlife, such as fish, mammals, reptiles, birds, insects, or plants. Books, computers, cameras, and microscopes are all necessary research equipment. There may be tanks containing minibeasts, and aquariums with fish and frogs. In one corner there is usually a blackboard, where the scientists record new species that are identified.

The main aim of most expeditions is to record biodiversity—the variety of life in the rain forest. Many parts of the Amazon are threatened by forest clearing, logging, mining, and other development that destroys the environment. If scientists can prove that a region is rich in wildlife, the government is more likely to agree to protect the area by making it into a reserve or national park.

Most life in a rain forest is found high in the air, in the canopy. But until recently, we knew little about life in this layer because it was so difficult to get there. Now scientists explore life in the treetops using equipment such as cranes, observation towers, hot air balloons, and even small unmanned airplanes called drones.

The most common way to explore life in the canopy is to rig a walkway. This looks like a rope bridge stretching between trees. There is usually a rope rail so you won't fall even if you lose your balance. To reach the walkway, you have to climb a rope using special climbing equipment. Wearing a hard hat and a climbing harness, you step into a sling. You then use sliding clips to lever yourself upward. These clips glide smoothly up the rope, then lock to hold you safely in position. Slowly, you inch higher and higher, and finally you reach a little platform at one end of the walkway. Climbing straight up the rope is a huge effort, so you'll probably need a rest before you start work!

High in the canopy, there are many dangers. One false move could be fatal. Scientists keep a careful watch for snakes, as well as stinging insects such as wasps and bees. These insects nest high in trees, but the nests can be well hidden. If you disturb one of these nests, the insects could swarm out and attack you, so you need to be on your guard.

Every level in the forest teems with life, from minibeasts right up to large predators such as jaguars. Many of these creatures blend in so well with the forest that they are hard to see even if you are really close. This vine snake is very hard to spot, but luckily it isn't dangerous.

However, many creeping or slithering creatures are armed with poison, such as centipedes and scorpions. Many snakes have very dangerous venom. The skin of some brightly colored frogs contains a poison so deadly that forest people use it to tip their darts and arrows when they go hunting. Big, hairy spiders called tarantulas can shoot hairs that stick into your skin and cause pain and irritation.

Even in the water you are not safe. Piranhas are small fish with razor-sharp teeth. If an animal falls into the water, the fish can strip its flesh in minutes. The world's largest snake, the anaconda, also lives in rivers. It kills its prey by wrapping its coils around it and then squeezing so its victim cannot breathe.

It's easy to get lost in the rain forest. There are very few landmarks and the trees often look similar. Streams, large trees, and thorn bushes block the way, which makes it hard to move in a straight line. In the rainy season, paths turn to mud and you may have to wade in waist-high water.

Scientists often hire local guides to scout paths through the forest. The guides hack back plants using large knives called machetes, but the jungle grows back quickly. Paths can disappear in just a week! People have gotten lost for hours or even days after taking just a few steps off the path.

For this reason, whenever you go walking in a rain forest or even in a local wood, take a compass. The red, magnetic needle on a compass points to north. From this you can work out the other compass directions. Using a map with a compass allows you to follow a route even through dense forest. Perhaps even more importantly, it shows you which way to go when you turn around and head for home.

Why is it easy to get lost in the rain forest?

Scientists who study insects are called entomologists. "Entom" comes from the Greek for insect, while "ologist" means someone who studies science. You might think that entomologists would use fancy equipment to study insects in a rain forest. In fact, they use a few simple bits of equipment that you can either make yourself or buy very cheaply. You can use the same equipment to study bugs in your backyard.

Scientists study small creatures in the leaf litter using a square frame called a quadrat. The expert sets the frame on the ground, then carefully investigates all the minibeasts inside. He or she identifies each bug and then counts the numbers of each species.

You can use the same technique to study bugs at home. You will need four tent pegs, string, and a tape measure. Measure out and peg a 3-foot (1 m) square on the ground. Gently transfer insects into a glass jar while you look at them with a magnifying glass. A guidebook can help you identify them. Always release the bugs when you have finished.

Entomologists also use sweep nets to capture flying insects such as butterflies. The fine mesh does not hurt the insects, which flutter away as soon as they are set free. At night, a lamp and a mesh net are used to study moths, which are attracted to light.

Pitfall traps are used to examine creepy-crawlies. These are small cups set in the ground, usually with loose-fitting lids to keep the rain out. The tasty bait attracts the bugs, which then slide down the smooth sides of the cup to the bottom.

CAMP MAP & RULES

DO...

- Wear insect repellent and cover body to protect against insect bites.
- Check for scorpions and other creatures before putting on boots and clothing.
- Boil water to ensure that it is safe for drinking.
- Clean and sterilize cuts and scratches to guard against infection.
- Keep food in watertight containers beyond the reach of animals.

DON'T...

- Don't touch the forest creatures, especially hairy or slithery ones.
- Beware of brightly colored animals because they may be poisonous.
- Never reach into dark holes or crevices.
- Don't swim far out in the river. There may be dangerous animals, such as piranhas, caiman, and anacondas (water snakes).
- Don't pollute streams and rivers.

hammock

rain forest

path

toilet

AMAZON RIVER

N

cook's storage

mess tent

storage

laboratory

generator

JUNGLE SURVIVAL MANUAL
LEARN TO USE A COMPASS

COMPASS DIRECTIONS

First you must know your directions: **N**orth, **E**ast, **S**outh, and **W**est. These directions are constant, no matter where you are. They can also be combined to become northeast, southeast, southwest, and northwest. You can compare the compass directions to numbers on a clock.

This phrase is a useful way to remember the directions: **N**ever **E**at **S**limy **W**orms

Direction of travel arrow:
fixed to the baseplate.

Magnetic needle:
colored end always points north and white end always points south.

Compass dial:
rotating dial with compass directions and 360º marked around the edge.

Orienting arrow:
fixed to the point on the compass dial labeled north.

READING A COMPASS

How to take a basic compass reading to find out in which direction you are traveling.

1 Hold the compass at waist height. Do not tilt it. Make sure the direction of travel arrow points toward where you are going.

2 Turn the compass dial so that the colored end of the magnetic needle is on N for North, to correspond with the orienting arrow.

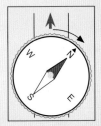

3 The direction of travel arrow will now point to the direction on the compass that you are traveling—in this example, northwest.

TAKING A BEARING

Bearings are used to find the way from one place to another. If you take a bearing when you set off, you will know that to get back, you need to go in the exact opposite direction—turning the dial 180°—to retrace your route.

97

JUNGLE SURVIVAL MANUAL

FIRST AID KIT

A good medical kit is vital on jungle expeditions. Make sure you know how to use it! You will also need vaccinations for tropical diseases and antimalarial pills.

> **Tip: AVOID INFECTION**
> Bacteria thrive in rain forests. Even minor cuts and scratches can easily become infected. Clean and sterilize all wounds using antiseptic wipes.

Pack a range of useful remedies and preventive medications.

sunscreen

calamine lotion

acetaminophen or other painkiller

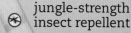 jungle-strength insect repellent

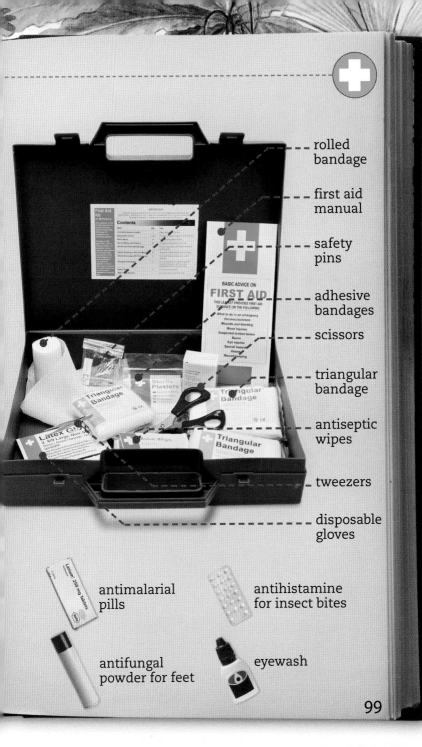

rolled bandage

first aid manual

safety pins

adhesive bandages

scissors

triangular bandage

antiseptic wipes

tweezers

disposable gloves

antimalarial pills

antihistamine for insect bites

antifungal powder for feet

eyewash

CHAPTER 7

CONSERVING RAIN FOREST BUGS

Rain forest bugs face many threats in the wild. But the biggest threat of all comes from people. In many parts of the Amazon, animals such as insects are threatened because their homes in the rain forests are being cut down.

This is called deforestation, and it is happening for several reasons. Logging is now an important industry in the Amazon. Huge swathes of forest have been felled for their valuable lumber, which is used to make houses and furniture. Wood is also pulped to make paper and burned as fuel. People may clear forest land to make way for fields, plantations, and cattle ranches. Other areas are bulldozed to mine gold, drill for oil, or build dams to produce electricity.

Seventy years ago, if you flew over the Amazon, you would have seen unbroken forest stretching to the horizon. Now many areas have been cleared. Red dirt roads cut through the forest, and smoke rises here and there.

When loggers arrive in a remote part of the forest, the peace is shattered. The whine of chainsaws fills the air. Mighty trees groan and come crashing to the ground. Bulldozers gouge dirt roads so trucks can remove the lumber. Soon, a leafy part of the forest that was home to millions of creatures is gone forever. In its place is a barren wasteland dotted with tree stumps and piles of woodchips.

In some parts of the Amazon, towns and villages have sprung up to house people who have moved from distant cities. In the last fifty years or so, cities on the coasts of South America have grown quickly and become overcrowded. The governments of rain forest nations often encourage city dwellers to move to the rain forest and become farmers. The newcomers clear land for farming, but the forest soil is too poor to grow crops or ranch cattle. After a few years, the settlers move on and clear a new patch of forest. Little by little, the rain forest is nibbled away.

THREATS TO THE AMAZON RAIN FOREST

The Amazon rain forest is unique. About a tenth of the world's birds, fish, frogs, and mammals are found here, and huge numbers of species are still to be discovered. Yet this precious habitat is disappearing quickly. Scientists estimate that an area the size of three football fields is lost every minute.

Amazon Gallery

Milk frog

Pink river dolphin

Toucan

Caiman

Black panther

Main threats to the Amazon

- Deforestation by legal and illegal logging companies. The trees are used for lumber and fuel.
- Forest clearance to make way for farms, roads, expanding towns, and dams.
- Mining for precious metals and drilling for oil.

Deforestation

What can be done to help?

- Wildlife organizations work alongside governments and local people to halt the destruction and preserve the forest.
- Experts record the unique wildlife of a region in a bid to protect large areas of untouched forest.

 About half of the precious forest that remains could be lost in the next 20 years if we don't take action now!

105

When rain forests are cut down, wildlife suffers. Animals have nowhere to live, and few plants survive, so there is little for them to eat. Scientists warn that forest destruction threatens tens of thousands of different plants and animals worldwide—including thousands of insects and other minibeasts that haven't even been discovered yet.

Deforestation is not the only threat that comes from people. Beautiful bugs such as butterflies are also prized by collectors. Poachers track them down and capture them in nets.

In days gone by, butterfly collectors wanted an example of every species to add to their collection. Fewer people collect insects in this way today, but butterflies are still targeted by hunters. They are killed, pinned to boards or plates, and sold as souvenirs. Insects are also used to make jewelry such as earrings, pendants, and brooches.

Unfortunately, it is usually the largest and most beautiful butterflies that are hunted. Morpho butterflies are probably the most spectacular insects of the Amazon. There are over 30 different species—the largest morphos measure 8 inches (20 cm) across their outstretched wings. Male morphos have wings of the deepest blue, which shimmer in the sunlight. These insects look like jewels, and indeed, they are often used to make jewelry or sold as souvenirs. So many morphos have been killed that these insects—which were once commonly seen in the Amazon—are now a much rarer sight.

So what can be done to protect butterflies like morphos? Scientists report endangered species to wildlife organizations. One international organization produces a list of all the animals that are in danger of dying out in rain forests and other places. Many countries have now banned trade in rare species.

Unfortunately, the rarer the insect, the higher the price it can fetch on the illegal market. Rare butterflies are still caught by poachers, who sell them to illegal dealers, who in turn try to sell them secretly for thousands of dollars.

Luckily, there is another way of protecting rare insects. Endangered butterflies are bred and reared on special farms. The breeders sell some of their young insects to collectors and souvenir-makers. This helps reduce the demand for wild butterflies, and so cuts down on poaching. Wildlife organizations may also buy the insects and then release them in the forest to boost the numbers of butterflies breeding in the wild.

As well as protecting rare species, it is also vital to protect the forest in which they live. Deforestation affects rain forests worldwide. Only 150 years ago, rain forests covered 12 percent of Earth's dry land. Now they cover less than six percent. If the destruction continues, there could be little forest left by 2050.

The good news is that governments, wildlife organizations, and ordinary people around the world are now working to protect rain forests. One way of doing this is to set up reserves and national parks. In the last 20 years, some large areas in the Amazon have been protected in this way. Parks and reserves attract tourists, who bring in cash that helps to pay for conservation.

Rain forests can be managed sustainably by planting new trees to replace the few selected for logging and harvesting forest produce such as fruits and nuts without cutting down trees.

Protecting land and managing forests sustainably are two important ways of making sure that these precious forests survive for years to come. Wildlife such as insects and other minibeasts must also be preserved, so that everywhere you look, bugs will still be crawling, hopping, and fluttering through the forest.

What are some ways that rain forests can be protected?

BUSH CRICKET

Also known as a cicada, bush crickets live in many parts of the world. In fact, there are more than 6,000 different species. Some male bush crickets produce a loud chirping sound to attract a mate.

Collecting Minibeasts

As all young entomologists know, there are dozens of ways to catch little creatures. These are three of the most effective ways. Use a magnifying glass to study the minibeasts.

 WHEN YOU HAVE FINISHED, MAKE SURE TO RELEASE THE CREATURES WHERE YOU FOUND THEM!

1 BEATING TRAY

Aim: to catch tree-dwelling insects and other bugs
You need: tray with sheet of white paper
Method: hold the tray under a low, leafy branch of a tree. Hit the branch several times with a stick. Use your beating tray to catch the insects that tumble out of the tree.

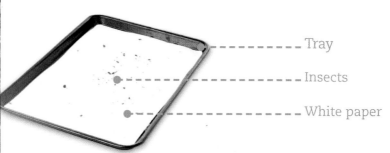

Tray

Insects

White paper

2 AERIAL NET

Aim: to catch flying insects such as butterflies

You need: butterfly net

Method: gently sweep the net in a figure eight. Flip the net over to trap the insects, and reverse to release. The fine mesh should not harm the insects.

∟ Butterfly net

3 PITFALL TRAP

Aim: to catch ground-dwelling insects, and also spiders, centipedes, millipedes, and other minibeasts

You need: cup or jar with bait such as banana or dry cat food; large stones; piece of wood or other cover

Method: dig a hole in the soil. Put some bait in the cup or jar, then place it in the hole. Position large stones on either side of the trap and cover with the wood to keep out the rain. The bugs will fall into the trap. Check traps at least twice a day.

Lid

Large stones

Cup/jar

Bait

Bug Habitats

If you want to hunt for bugs to study, there are many places you can look. Different kinds of insects live in different habitats. A habitat is more than just a home. It gives the insect everything it needs to survive, including food and the right conditions for mating and breeding.

FRESHWATER
Many insects live on the surface of the water, swim below it, or fly above it. Dip a net in to observe the insects, but some bite so don't touch!

LEAF LITTER
A pile of rotting leaves is a good place to find creepy crawlies such as this wood louse.

IMPORTANT!
Take care when lifting up branches or stones, because animals beneath them can sometimes bite or sting. It's best to lift stones with a stick.

Indoors

You can find insects indoors too, including temporary visitors such as flies, as well as spiders and some types of ants. Spiders are useful because they keep other insects under control.

TREES AND SHRUBS
There's plenty for insects to eat in trees and shrubs. Look hard to find caterpillars, crickets, or aphids.

GRASS AND FLOWERS
Butterflies and bees feed on the nectar in flowers. You're most likely to spot them on warm, sunny days.

WALLS AND PAVING
In warm weather, you may see minibeasts on walls or paving, or hiding in the cracks.

Housefly

House spider

Silverfish

Compost Critters

Make a habitat for a variety of small creatures in your garden compost bin. The compost will warm up and rot down, making a perfect home for creepy-crawlies. Tiny minibeasts will live on the decaying plant matter, while larger creatures will feed on the smaller ones.

Compost bin

Frogs and toads may visit to feed on insects, slugs, and snails.

Small mammals love a compost snack too.

Spiders eat smaller insects.

Centipedes eat small soil animals and slugs. Millipedes eat mostly decaying plant matter.

Ants feed on seeds and will often make a nest in a compost bin.

Big bugs and insects feed on small bugs and insects.

Earwigs like potato peelings, cauliflowers, celery, and old grapes!

Compost mites

Wood lice eat decaying plant matter.

Earthworms

Worms, along with mites and fungus, break down leaves and paper.

Snails eat leaves and other plant matter.

- ✓ Plant clippings
- ✓ Dry leaves and twigs
- ✓ Grass cuttings
- ✓ Dead heads of flowers
- ✓ Tea bags and coffee grounds
- ✓ Paper towels and napkins
- ✓ Annual weeds
- ✓ Straw and hay
- ✓ Broken egg shells
- ✓ Corn cobs and stalks
- ✓ Vegetable peelings
- ✓ Shredded newspaper
- ✓ Fruit skin and apple cores
- ✓ Scrunched up cardboard

Compost materials

Compost waste can generally be divided into greens and browns. The greens are soft, sappy materials that rot quickly, while the browns are drier materials. On their own, greens would produce a foul-smelling sludge, so make sure to include more browns than greens in your compost. Minibeasts thrive on this too!

BUG HUNT

Now it's your turn to be a bug hunter!

The insects pictured at the bottom of these pages are hiding in the jungle, along with a crested forest toad. Can you spot them all in this picture of the Amazon Rain Forest?

Look carefully—the insects are well camouflaged!

Stick insect

Praying mantis

Brown grasshopper

Moth

Leaf bush cricket

Cockroach

BIG BUG QUIZ

See if you can find the answers to these questions about what you have read.

1. What does the word "arthropod" mean?

2. How many legs does an arachnid have?

3. What is the middle section of an adult insect called?

4. What is an insect's proboscis?

5. What is the world's deadliest animal?

6. How high can a flea jump?

7. What is the name of the insect group that butterflies and moths belong to?

8. In flies, where is the sense of smell located?

9. What do leafcutter ants eat?

10. On which continent is the Amazon River?

11. How long is the Amazon River?

12. In which layer of the rain forest is plant and animal life most plentiful?

13. What are larvae of Alder moths disguised as?

14. What do entomologists study?

Answers on page 125.

GLOSSARY

Abdomen
Rear section of an insect's body.

Antennae
Long feelers on an insect's head, used for touch, smell, and taste.

Arthropods
Group of small creatures with a hard outer skeleton, including insects, spiders, scorpions, and centipedes.

Ascender
Metal clamp used as a climbing aid.

Bearing
Direction in which a person is headed.

Biodiversity
Variety of life found in a habitat such as a rain forest.

Caste (insect)
Social insect that has a specific role in the colony.

Conservation
Protection of nature.

Deforestation
Cutting down a forest for lumber or to clear land.

Drone
Male insect such as a bee.

Entomologist
Scientist studying insects.

Incomplete metamorphosis
Three-stage life cycle.

Larva (plural: larvae)
Young insect.

Metamorphosis
Four-stage life cycle.

Nymph
Young insect with a three-stage life cycle.

Predator
Creature that hunts other creatures for food.

Prey
Creature hunted by predators.

Proboscis
Tubelike mouthparts of insects such as butterflies.

Pupa
Stage between a caterpillar and an adult in insects that undergo metamorphosis.

Sterile
Unable to lay eggs.

Thorax
Middle section of an insect's body.

Answers to the Big Bug Quiz:
1. Joint-legged; **2.** Eight; **3.** Thorax; **4.** Tubelike mouthparts; **5.** *Anopheles* mosquito (because it transmits malaria); **6.** eight inches (130 times its own height); **7.** *Lepidoptera*; **8.** Feet; **9.** Special fungus; **10.** South America; **11.** 4,000 miles (6,440 km); **12.** Canopy; **13.** Bird droppings; **14.** Insects.

INDEX

About the Author

Dr. Jen Green is a full-time writer, specializing in history, geography, nature, environment, and earth science. She has written many books on bugs, rain forest, and survival. She received her doctorate from Sussex University in England, and then worked in publishing for many years. Now with a writing career spanning 20 years, she has published more than 300 books, many of which have been translated. She has also written many articles for encyclopedias and journals. She lives in a village in England's Sussex Downs with her dog.

About the Consultant

Dr. Linda Gambrell, Distinguished Professor of Education at Clemson University, has served as President of the National Reading Conference, the College Reading Association, and the International Reading Association. She is also reading consultant for the *DK Readers*.

Have you read these other great books from DK?

DK ADVENTURES

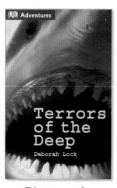

Discover the wonders of the world's deepest, darkest ocean trench.

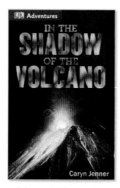

Mount Vesuvius erupts in this adventure. Will Carlo escape?

It's a life-or-death adventure as the gang searches for a new home planet.

Chase twisters in Tornado Alley in this pulse-racing action adventure.

Discover what life for pilots, women, and children was like during WWII.

Emma adores horses. Will her wish come true at a riding camp?

5